The Aquinas Lecture, 1957

ST. THOMAS
AND
THE FUTURE
OF METAPHYSICS

Under the Auspices of the Aristotelian Society
of Marquette University

By

JOSEPH OWENS, C.Ss.R., M.S.D.

SECOND PRINTING

MARQUETTE UNIVERSITY PRESS
MILWAUKEE
1973

Prefatory

The Aristotelian Society of Marquette University each year invites a scholar to deliver a lecture in honor of St. Thomas Aquinas. Customarily delivered on a Sunday close to March 7, the feast day of the Society's patron saint, the lectures are called the Aquinas lectures.

In 1957 the Aquinas lecture, "St. Thomas and the Future of Metaphysics," was given by Fr. Joseph Owens, C.Ss.R.

Fr. Owens received the Licentiate in Mediaeval Studies in 1946 and the Doctorate of Mediaeval Studies in Philosophy in 1951, both from the Pontifical Institute of Mediaeval Studies in Toronto.

He taught at the Academia Alfonsiana in Rome 1952-1953, and at Assumption University at Windsor, Ontario, in 1954. Since then he has been teaching at the Pontifical Institute of Mediaeval Studies in Toronto where he is associate professor of philosophy, and also at St. Alphonsus Seminary, Woodstock, Ont.

Fr. Owens is the author of *The Doctrine of Being in the Aristotelian Metaphysics* (Toronto, Pontifical Institute of Mediaeval Studies, 1951).

He has also written the following articles:

"Up to What Point is God Included in the Metaphysics of Duns Scotus?" *Mediaeval Studies,* X (1948) 163-177;

"The Reality of the Aristotelian Separate Movers," *The Review of Metaphysics,* III (1950) 319-337;

"Theodicy, Natural Theology and Metaphysics," *The Modern Schoolman,* XXVIII (1951) 126-137;

"The Conclusion of the *Prima Via,*" *The Modern Schoolman,* XXX (1952-53) 33-53; 109-121; 203-215;

"The Special Characteristic of the Scotistic Proof that God Exists," *Analecta Gregoriana,* LXVII (1954) 311-327;

"The Causal Proposition—Principle or Conclusion?" *The Modern Schoolman,* XXXII (1955) 159-171; 257-270; 323-339;

"A Note on the Approach to Thomistic Metaphysics," *The New Scholasticism,* XXVIII (1954) 454-476;

"The Intelligibility of Being," *Gregorianum,* XXXVI (1955) 169-193;

"Our Knowledge of Nature," *Proceedings of the American Catholic Philosophical Association,* XXIX (1955) 63-86.

To these the Aristotelian Society takes pleasure in adding *St. Thomas and the Future of Metaphysics.*

St. Thomas and the Future of Metaphysics

The Problem of the Future of Metaphysics

A witness of the canonization process of St. Thomas Aquinas testified to what may seem a rather amazing statement made by Albert the Great. After the death of St. Thomas, Albert as an old man had undertaken the long journey to Paris to defend the memory of his younger confrere. On his return to Cologne he wanted to have all the works of Brother Thomas read to him in a set order; and he concluded his encomia on them by saying that the same Brother Thomas had in his writings put an end to everybody's labors right up to the end of the world, and that from now on all further work would be without purpose![1]

Can one find anywhere a grain of salt that might render such a statement palatable? Certainly history tears it to shreds when it is understood in any obvious sense. At its face value, it would imply that all intellectual work of the kind undertaken by St. Thomas Aquinas had come to an end with his death. Any further attempts at development would be a waste of time. The sum total of human intellectual achievement would have been already attained and would remain complete for admiration and respect but not open to progress or change. Like the Platonic world of perfect being in the impasse to which it seemed to have been brought by the description of the Eleatic Stranger,[2] Thomistic doctrine would stand there rigid for all time in solemn immobility, aloof from the ever-changing intellectual life of mankind. Metaphysics, like all other parts of the Thomistic doctrine, would have its history completed. It would be something entirely of the past. It would have no future, and you would be spared the trouble of listening to a lecture on this afternoon's topic.

However, nearly seven hundred years of variegated doctrinal history have blossomed since the reported statement of St. Albert. Even at first glance the wide panorama shows clearly enough that human intellectual achievement did not at all cease with the death of St. Thomas. Rather, in all fields there has been continued and intensive development, generally outside the framework of the thirteenth century Thomistic structure, and in most cases with startling and undreamt of success. History denies emphatically that St. Thomas in his writings has put an end to all intellectual labors.

In giving his testimony, the witness, Bartholomew of Capua, undoubtedly had in mind the whole fabric of Christian doctrine, as found sketched in St. Paul, developed in St. Augustine, and brought to outstanding splendor in St. Thomas Aquinas. In this sense and in this succession Bartholomew went on immediately to quote the archbishop of Naples, Blessed James of Viterbo, as believing that Brother Thomas would have no successor till the end of time.[3] In point of fact, St. Thomas lived quite close to the end of the long period in human history in which one man could come fairly close to assimilating the greater part of all the learning that his epoch regarded as important. In this sense, possibly, St. Thomas might be viewed as the last in a certain definite line, somewhat as the ancient Greek biographers loved to arrange their philosophers in closed dynastic successions. But many different subjects had been incorporated into the Christian wisdom of St. Thomas' day. The question of how final his own treatment was in any of these matters has to be dealt with separately for each individual field. Only one such area, that of metaphysics, claims our attention this afternoon. What possible bearing could Albert's reported judgment have upon the history and the future of metaphysics? Has it any basis whatsoever in actual fact? Is there any sense, however remote, in which it may be looked upon as true in regard to the achievement of St. Thomas Aquinas in the realm of metaphysical thought?

Certainly there is the obvious historical sense in which that judgment is definitely false. The broad and intricate tapestry of intellectual endeavor which has been woven from the last quarter of the thirteenth century to our own day, shows strikingly enough that the accomplishment of St. Thomas Aquinas did not bring to an end the labors of the metaphysicians. It seems, indeed, to indicate anything but that. Even within the orbit of the Thomistic interpreters, no such finality is apparent. Among those who claim to be explaining the doctrine contained in the Thomistic texts, there has in

fact been endless disagreement throughout the centuries, and perhaps never more
so than at the present time. The Thomistic
writings, far from closing all metaphysical
efforts, have rather given rise even within
their own boundaries to intense and cen-
turies-long labor in the attempt to arrive
at their authentic meaning. Moreover, of
its very nature, as the Aquinas lecturer of
seven years ago pointed out to you, Thomistic metaphysics is of such a character that
it can never become closed and final. On
the contrary, it remains open to all advancing insight into reality.[4] It is a doctrine
that has to be re-thought and re-lived
through the changing problems and differ-
ing outlook of each succeeding generation.

Outside the ambit of Thomistic
thought, the disagreement is, of course,
still more striking. Far from accepting
Thomistic doctrine as final and obligatory,
the course of metaphysical endeavors has
for the vastly greater part proceeded from
starting-points that are not the principles

of St. Thomas. It has developed through a wide variety of channels, and in most instances has arrived at conclusions that have little similarity to those of Aquinas. Giles of Rome, Henry of Ghent, John Duns Scotus, to mention only a few names in the epoch immediately following his death, pursued radically different paths of metaphysical thinking. With the Cartesians the divergence becomes yet more apparent, as ideas instead of things formed the starting-point of metaphysical procedure. For a brief moment the new chaos seemed to become systematized in the academic achievement of Christian Wolff. The general metaphysical treatment was named ontology and was allotted the rather jejune task of studying the most abstract[5] human notions. The concepts of God and of the rational soul were deliberately excluded from the general science and along with that of the cosmos were assigned to three parallel branches of special metaphysics, all three having the status of particular sciences. This flimsy Wolffian structure tumbled to the ground under the shattering critique of Kant. Kant isolated the urge toward metaphysical thinking as a natural disposition of the human mind, but a disposition which when cultivated could result only in an inescapable illusion of transcendental make-believe.

Hegel, appalled by the strange spectacle of an otherwise educated people without metaphysics, like an elaborately decorated temple without object of cult,[6] endeavored to restore the ancient science to its appropriate sanctuary. But in this attempt metaphysics became a logic of ideas, resulting in the grandiose idealistic systems of the nineteenth century. Those systems, like the sun-maidens of Parmenides, guided the chariots of metaphysical thought along heights far removed from the paths of ordinary mortals. The reaction of an age aglow with the warm triumphs of experimental science was the attitude of positivism. Metaphysics was reduced to the function of a youthful and immature stage of human development, something to be totally abandoned now that maturity has been reached. Pragmatism dismissed it cavalierly as a pastime for the tender-minded, with no place in the tough-minded pursuits of modern life. Logical empiricism culminated this trend by showing how on the positivistic basis it was sheer non-sense. Yet the void created by the positivistic outlook had to be filled. New approaches like phenomenology and existentialism and logical analysis endeavored to provide a satisfactory basis for human thinking, while contemporary types of metaphysics turned their backs upon the study of being and sought to find the core of reality through an intuition deeper than intellectual manipulation, or remained content with a mere cataloguing of the ultimate presuppositions of individuals or definite historical groups.

Certainly, the work of St. Thomas Aquinas has not put an end to all labors in the realm of metaphysics! Rather, the difficulty today for metaphysics is to take even the first step toward a proper place in the advanced and complicated culture which is ours. You may remember well enough the crocodile tears that ooze through the Kantian lament over the sad and lowly status to which the once great queen of the sciences had been seemingly forever reduced.[7] Since that time, like a challenger whom repeated knock-outs and technical knock-outs cannot discourage, metaphysics has come back again and again to battle for its ancient crown. Just at present there seems a better founded hope than at any time during the last few centuries that the science is at least taking its first sure step toward an acknowledged place in the intellectual world. During the past decade periodicals devoted expressly to metaphysics have been founded. Books dealing with its problems have been increasing in output and circulation. At the last international congress of philosophy, held in Brussels in 1953, no one had to apologize for introducing metaphysical topics, and in fact a considerable portion of the papers and discussions bore on such subjects.

However, at that same congress a speaker from the floor called sobering attention to what little impression a gathering of philosophers from all continents was making upon contemporary interest. It attracted slight notice in the press, it was exercising no discernible influence whatsoever on the trends of thought and activity in the world about it. Hardly any one outside those professionally interested even knew that the congress was going in. This lack of interest and concern holds all the more when it is brought to bear upon the case of metaphysics. Most university graduates today are at best only vaguely familiar with the name. There seems no exaggeration in suggesting that one could register next Sunday in the "What's My Line" program as a "metaphysician" and enjoy a one hundred per cent chance of escaping detection!

A suitable place for metaphysics in our general culture is, evidently, still a matter of the future. The labors of metaphysicians to attain that status for their science is quite obviously only beginning. There is accordingly ample occasion for inquiring whether a proper place for metaphysics may be envisaged in the culture that is shaping before us today, and what part the doctrine of St. Thomas Aquinas is able to play in securing that place for the science. It is not a question of attempting to prophesy the future. Too many contingent and uncontrollable factors, not excluding the possibility of atomic war, will be at work. Rather, the problem is to examine what role metaphysics is able to play in the world as we know it and as you, for instance, in your university are working toward shaping it, and what need there is for the presence and activity and general acceptance of metaphysics in such a world.

The Nature of Metaphysics

The first step one would like to take in facing such a problem is to get a fairly clear conception of what metaphysics is. Any one engaged in metaphysics, either as student or professor or writer, is occasionally asked a simple and obvious but still perplexing question. When some one inquires what your work is and you answer "Metaphysics," the first reaction is usually a rather surprised "Oh!" Then, hesitatingly, comes the inevitable question: "But what is metaphysics?" You try to answer, and you find that you are the person who is really embarrassed. It is easy enough to reply that for Plato metaphysics would be the dialectic of the Ideas, that for Aristotle it is the science of the separate substances, that for St. Thomas it is a study of things from the viewpoint of their existential act, for Bradley a pursuit of the Absolute, for Collingwood the discovery of ultimate presuppositions, and so on. But you realize that your answer sounds very academic. It does not put your point across, and moreover it is not what your inquirer wants. Like Socrates he is not interested in your indicating to him this or that example of the notion. He wants to know what the virtue itself is. He has little concern with this or that instance of metaphysical undertaking. He wants to know in what metaphysics itself consists.

Faced with the question in that perspective, the answer becomes surprisingly difficult. Aristotle in the opening book of the *Metaphysics* envisioned the same query with the speculations of his predecessors before his mind's eye. He answered quite vaguely for the moment that wisdom is the science of the ultimate principles and causes.[8] This definition has not passed unchallenged. For some, metaphysics does not come under the designation of "science" at all; rather, like philosophy in general, it is explicitly set apart from and contrasted with science. For others, the notion of "causes" may not enter into the

definition. Even "principles" may be too
definite. The concept may be watered
down to "presuppositions" or "assump-
tions." However, the notion of "ultimate"
does seem common enough in some way
to all conceptions of metaphysics. Whatever else one may consider metaphysics to
be, it will at least be seeking an explanation or a description that is in the broadest
manner the ultimate possible to the un-
aided human faculties. It will be a type of
cognition that seeks to go beyond and back
of the knowledge given in the other pursuits. That notion of going "beyond" the
sciences of the visible world seems in fact
to be implicit in even the very name
"metaphysics." Long thought to have originated in a mere historical accident, because Andronicus of Rhodes in the first
century B.C. placed the treatises on the
Aristotelian primary philosophy *after* those
on the philosophy of nature, the name has
been more recently traced by scholars far
beyond Andronicus back to the last quar-

ter of the third century, within a hundred years from Aristotle's death.[9] Whether it originally indicated that the metaphysical treatises were to be studied *after* the physical treatises, according to the necessary Aristotelian procedure, or whether it meant that metaphysics studied things which are *beyond* the physical order, is still unknown. But in either case it denoted for the Peripatetics the science that reached back of the physical treatment of the universe and studied the separate substances. It was defined as a theology in this sense. The separate substances, substances apart from or beyond the world of nature, beyond the world of matter and form, were for Aristotle the highest and ultimate causes of the universe. Knowledge of such causes was therefore the highest and ultimate knowledge possible. Contemplation of such substances, the pursuit of metaphysics, was the supreme goal of human life, both social and individual. It was indeed attainable by men only in rare moments and for brief intervals, but it was worth subordinating to its attainment all individual and social activity. It was the supreme end of human life. It was life at its highest and best.

The place of metaphysics in this Aristotelian conception is easy enough to understand. It was the science that gave knowledge of things which could be reached by no other human study. Separate substance, the summit and fullness of intellection and intelligibility, was the highest possible object of human thought; and in knowing it man attained his beatitude. Little wonder, then, that in the Aristotelian tradition metaphysics occupied the highest place among the sciences. What it treated of was very definite—the immaterial substances, the world beyond the material order. It was the study of being simply as being, for in the immaterial substances there was no principle of change, no material element which could allow any becoming and so introduce the classical Greek opposite of being. It attained being without any possibility of becoming, being simply as being.

The metaphysicians of the middle ages were ready enough to characterize metaphysics as the science of being as being. But they could not equate being as being with the being of any separate substances. They could not define metaphysics outright as the science of spiritual beings. They were keenly interested in the knowledge of the spiritual beings revealed in their sacred books—God, the angels, and the subsistent human soul. But these differed too widely in their natures to be described sufficiently by any one formula like being as being, after the fashion of the Aristotelian separate substances. The divine nature, moreover, could hardly be conceived by them as the subject of a specifically human science. Hence God and the other spiritual substances were not looked upon as the subject of metaphysics by the mediaevals, except in the case of

Averroes who clung to the letter of the Aristotelian text. Later, in modern times, being as being or common being became the general notion of being, abstracting from all its differences. The problem which arose was to find any content in such a notion, that would allow it to function as the object of a science. Finally it was eliminated entirely from the definition of metaphysics, or declared non-sensical by the very fact that it purported to go beyond the sensible order.

From all this survey, apparently, no very clear answer emerges to the embarrassing question of what metaphysics is. Vaguely, one can say that it deals with something ultimate in the broadest sense, and perhaps also that it treats of something beyond the obvious, beyond the limited knowledge of senses, beyond nature, when the term 'nature' is restricted to the material universe. Further than that, however, metaphysics can hardly be brought under a formula comprehensive enough to extend to all the various conceptions of it which history has unfolded. Whether one likes the prospect or not, if one wishes to work seriously toward a future for it, one has to select a definite type of metaphysics which will inevitably exclude other types of thought that have borne the name. At the present stage of the long history of metaphysical endeavor, if one is to start at all, one is left with the necessity of choosing a definite starting-point and aiming at definite objectives, and of adopting a procedure that really gives promise of attaining those objectives.

The Need for Metaphysical Thinking

In making such a choice, one has to have a motive, a purpose. What need can metaphysics fill in the culture that is developing around us? Why is there any call for a science that deals with the ultimate, a science of something beyond what is treated by logic and all the particular sciences? What advantages can there be to a civilization in having a metaphysics?

This requirement of a motive for making the choice brings up the second inevitable question that is asked about metaphysics, a question which at first sight may seem even meaner than the one about what the pursuit is. It is the question concerning the utility of the science. What use is metaphysics?

In the Aristotelian tradition the rather easy answer might be that metaphysics is of no use at all. It is above all use. It is an end and not a means. It is to be pursued for its own sake, and not for any utility that it may bring to the other interests of human life. Such an answer, however, will at most bring only an amused and skeptical smile from your inquirer. It can hardly be expected to make an impression upon a generation that has been moulded according to the norms of the Deweyite pursuit of the useful. But even aside from this contemporary attitude, it could scarcely be satisfying to any one grounded in the Christian outlook on things. From a Christian viewpoint God alone, possessed in the beatific vision, is the ultimate end of human life. A merely human science, like metaphysics, must in this conception play an ancillary role. It is to be pursued in so far as it is helpful toward attaining that ultimate end.

What utility can metaphysics have in this regard? What knowledge of ultimates, or of things beyond the range of the particular sciences, can be of real use here?

If one takes metaphysics in its Aristotelian conception, as the knowledge of the immaterial substances, or, if one wishes to go back to Plato's Dialectic, as knowledge of the unchangeable Ideas, one can get a hint of how a scientific cognition of the things beyond the sensible world may have a definite utility in a culture whose foundation is Christian. Transposed into the Christian background, the things beyond the sensible world are God, the angels, and the spiritual soul. These are accepted by the Christian on the strength

of divine revelation. Naturally, a desire
arises to know more about them. They are
proposed as truths by one's faith, but their
peculiar importance at once places them
as objects of inquiry for one's intellect.
Belief in God Who is the author of one's
being and the sovereign Lord to Whom
one is responsible for all one's actions, and
belief in a future eternal life to which all
one's conduct has to be directed, make a
tremendous difference in the over-all as
well as the day to day decisions of one's
life. It is but natural that one should yearn
to know as well as to believe such truths.
The natural desire toward scientific knowledge which Aristotle signalized in the
opening lines of the *Metaphysics*[10] extends
pre-eminently to knowledge of God and of
the soul. One would like to possess these
truths not merely on faith, nor just as
postulates of a morality ultimately based
on that faith, but as fully proven scientific
conclusions that can unhesitatingly take
their proper place in the vast body of

truths which a cultured intellect highly and rightly values under the name of science.

True, such scientific knowledge is not essential to salvation. It can function at best but as a condition. Other conditions can and for the immeasurably greater part do suffice. The trust in the word of parents and religious teachers, for instance, is sufficient to provide the necessary condition for the child's initial act of faith, and the supernatural faith so infused can be and regularly is abundantly sustained by devout religious practice. Yet to some minds, besides filling the natural desire to know, a scientific knowledge of God and the spiritual soul cannot but serve as a strong bulwark and as a deeply appreciated help in their intellectual inquiries and struggles. It has its place as an integral part of their intellectual life.

Moreover, it is not hard to imagine the difference there would be in living in a culture that accepted as beyond question a science that established the existence and attributes of God and the immortality of the human soul, as naturally as it accepts the theory of electrons and protons. The spectacle of acknowledged experts in their own particular sciences using their authority to spread popular confusion about God and the soul would be rendered absurd. On mention of those topics they would be obliged simply to refer to the authorities under whose scientific competence such subjects fall, just as the nuclear physicist would defer to the knowledge of the botanist regarding the habitat of a particular plant. It is not at all a question of "metaphysics for the millions"[11] in the impossible sense that every one should have an expert knowledge of the science. Rather, it would involve merely the general recognition of the status and authority of metaphysics as an established science, just as the structure of the galaxies is generally accepted by the millions who have no competence whatever is astronomy or celestial physics.

Nor is there any question of such knowledge supplying for the work of the theologian, the moralist, or the preacher. One hears often enough that the demonstrations of the existence of God have no power to influence those who do not already believe, and are superfluous for those who do—they have no power to move the heart. That is not at all the point. The work of the scientific inquirer, here as elsewhere, is to discover and set forth the process by which the conclusions follow inexorably from their evident starting-points. His task as such ends there. The function of appealing or persuading belongs to others.

The role of a scientific knowledge of God and the soul in a general culture is accordingly very modest, even though it is important. But modest as such a role may be, you will perhaps shrug your shoulders and say that in the practical world as we know it there is not the slightest chance in the foreseeable future that metaphysics will ever acquire any accepted status among the honored ranks of the acknowledged sciences. True, the prospect is difficult to imagine. But history plays strange tricks. Two years ago a nuclear physicist in a lecture at Toronto dwelt upon the tremendous potentialities of atomic energy for good and for evil, and concluded that the task of directing it to the welfare rather than the destruction of mankind lay with the political scientists. He added: "You may be surprised to hear me, a physical scientist, calling those fellows 'scientists'; but the new circumstances have made us see that their work is really scientific and they have a big job to do." That is but an indication that the narrow nineteenth century restriction of the time-honored notion of "science" is not something static and fixed forever, but is open to the changing circumstances and the progressive accomplishments of succeeding generations, and need not at all remain adverse to recognizing once again the type

of knowledge that in former times was regarded as science in the highest sense of
the term, once that science presents itself
in an acceptable and convincing form.

Finally, there is manifested repeatedly
in the history of human thought the long-
ing for a general science that will in some
satisfactory way assess the relative place of
each of the particular sciences and allow
the work of all to be seen in some kind of
unity and harmony. This will have to be a
science that regards all things from the
widest possible viewpoint, and so be able
to judge the respective functions of the
sciences which treat of particular groups
or aspects of things. Such a general science
would be able to show the limits and the
relative bearing of every science, itself not
excepted, and so would act as an antidote
against the temptation of the expert to in-
terpret everything merely from the restricted viewpoint of his own competence,
even though that competence be metaphysics itself. Such a general science alone

can satisfy, as far as is possible in this life, the unifying tendency of the human intellect, which is not content until it sees a universal principle of order in some way pervading all the objects that are presented to it. Only then is the order sought by speculative wisdom attained.

There, then, are the needs which are waiting to be filled by an appropriate metaphysics. What type of metaphysics will this be? Evidently one whose procedure is truly scientific, for on all points just sketched a properly scientific knowledge alone can meet the requirements. It calls for a procedure starting from what is self-evident to all, and advancing step by step along a path of rigorous rational demonstration to the conclusions that were implicitly contained in its premises. A metaphysics that aims to be an intuitive process beyond the reasoning of the intellect,[12] or a historical cataloguing of presuppositions,[13] or a type of literary creation in which prose borders on poetry,[14] obviously will not suffice for these needs, whatever merits such conceptions of metaphysics may otherwise have. The only kind of metaphysics that will fill these wants is a type that is objectively scientific, that is, which will present an organized body of reasoned knowledge communicable to all and not restricted to particular circumstances of person or time. True, such a metaphysics has to be a living and when fully developed a creative habit,[15] and so can live and function only in particular individuals. A habit, however, is specified by its object, and that object, in the case of a science, is something fixed in the nature of things and universally accessible to all.

The Contribution of St. Thomas

What prospects does the metaphysical doctrine of St. Thomas Aquinas offer toward meeting these requirements? Certainly no completely developed and finished metaphysics is to be expected in the writings of the great thirteenth century doctor. His metaphysical teachings are for the most part scattered throughout theological treatises or Aristotelian and other commentaries, and brought in only as occasion demanded. But may one hope to find at least the basic principles of a satisfactory metaphysics in the writings of St. Thomas? Have his metaphysical doctrines penetrated to a depth unknown to his predecessors, for example, to Plato, Aristotle and Plotinus? Have they reached a stratum beyond which no one since his time has been able to delve? Do the principles of St. Thomas finally put metaphysical thinking on the proper level and on the right path which it is meant to follow in seeking the ultimate? Is it in this sense that Albert's statement as reported by Bartholomew really has its bearing on the metaphysical accomplishment of the Angelic Doctor? Does the doctrine of St. Thomas finally ground metaphysical thinking on the basis which its nature requires, so that all further attempts in seeking such a foundation are in vain? Even though the work of developing that metaphysics may lie ahead, even though its penetration may be pushed ever deeper and deeper into reality, has it nevertheless at last found the fundamental starting-point and the appropriate procedure through which metaphysics can satisfactorily attain its objectives?

First of all, the metaphysical procedure found in the writings of St. Thomas presents itself explicitly as that of a science.[16] It starts from what is evident in every one's immediate experience of the visible and tangible world, in fact from what is most self-evident of all, namely that something exists. Into this basic and utterly self-evident premise does it ultimately resolve all its conclusions.[17] From this unshakeable starting-point does it proceed to its conclusions according to the rigorous technique of *propter quid*[18] reasoning, the most truly scientific type of thinking possible.

The metaphysical doctrine of St.

Thomas, then, explicitly lays claim to the procedure and the status of a true science. It aims expressly, moreover, at knowledge of God and the spiritual substances.[19] It purports to be a general science showing the universal order that pervades all the objects of human knowledge.[20] Such is its professed character. Does it, however, actually succeed in attaining these objectives? Can it accomplish satisfactorily a task in which so many other metaphysics, earlier and later, have proven themselves deficient?

Here the real difficulties begin. The problem of understanding the character of St. Thomas' metaphysical thought has been approached in various ways. The nineteenth century revival of interest in his achievement tended to regard it as a mediaeval Aristotelianism, explaining it in the light of the basic Aristotelian principles of *act and potency*, in accordance with the long tradition of the Thomistic commentators.[21] In the first two decades of the pres-

ent century there became apparent the
need of going beyond the Aristotelian
framework (though still remaining within
the orbit of the traditional commentators),
by proposing the *analogy of proper proportionality* as the key to understanding
the Thomistic metaphysical procedure.[22]
In the middle thirties came the trend to
look outside the time-honored commentators as well as the Aristotelian background,
and seek in the Platonic and Neo-Platonic
doctrines of *participation* the basis for a
more profound interpretation.[23]   Finally,
with the forties there has become domi-
nant the tendency to see in the *existential*
character of Thomistic metaphysics its
deepest and most proper feature,[24] which
alone can finally unlock the gates to the intellectual riches that for centuries have
been divined to lie behind its seemingly
innocent and commonplace yet highly en-
igmatic formulae.

Each of these successive stages in the
modern efforts at interpretation has played

an important part in penetrating further
and further toward the core of St. Thomas'
metaphysical doctrine. No one of them
can be neglected. Act and potency, analogy of proper proportionality, participation, the primacy of existential act, have
all proved necessary for understanding the
thought of the Angelic Doctor. No one of
them excludes the others. Rather, each requires all the others. In particular, the
most recent and deepest penetration, the
existential, cannot at all be understood
without a thorough grasp of the three preceding interpretations. The existential
viewpoint means that existence plays the
role of act in regard to a proper potency,
essence, and *thereby* attains absolute primacy in the thing. It requires that this relation of act and potency be understood as
only analogous to that of the Aristotelian
form and matter, and likewise as propor-
tional throughout the different orders of
being. It implies that existence subsists in
one being alone, and is *participated* analo-

gously as act by potency in all other things. The three previous viewpoints are accordingly included in the existential, and come to their full flower in it. Through it they grow to the maturity in which they can function freely as means of understanding the peculiarly proper movement of Thomistic metaphysics.

What is meant exactly by the existential interpretation of St. Thomas' doctrine? The term "existential" is quite evidently borrowed from the trend in modern thought that commenced with Kierkegaard and is so well known today through the work of men like Heidegger, Jasper, and Sartre. As in these writers, so in St. Thomas existence is seen in contrast to essence, and as having the absolute primacy over essence.[25] However, in St. Thomas this contrast does not fall between subjectivity and objectivity. Rather, the existence first known is that of external sensible objects. Existence is in this sense fully as objective as essence, and essence

likewise pertains as much to the subject as
to the object. In other words, "existence"
in the Thomistic doctrine bears no intrinsic
resemblance at all to what is meant by the
same term in the modern existentialists.
The only analogy that allows the same
name to denote both types of thinking is
that, in each, existence is given an absolute
priority over essence. Accordingly, the
standard themes of modern existentialism,
anguish, nausea, frustration, despair, and
so on, need not be looked for in the development of Thomistic thought.

What is meant, then, by "existence" in
the metaphysics of St. Thomas? Actually,
the word occurs but rarely in the volumin-
ous works of the Angelic Doctor.[26] The
regular term used by St. Thomas for the
notion is the Latin infinitive *esse*, to be.
It is perhaps best translated into English
by the participle "being."[27] The being of
a thing, according to the existentialist interpretation of the Thomistic doctrine, is
originally attained by the human intellect

not through any act of conceptualization, but only through the act of judging.[28] When a thing—for instance, a tree, a table, a stone—is presented to one's intellectual cognition, that thing is at once grasped in a two-fold way. It is attained according to its essence or nature by the act of conceptualization and, simultaneously, according to its being by the judgment. The intellect at the same time conceives *what* the thing is and judges *that* it exists.

Exactly what is attained by the intellect in judging that a thing exists? It is evidently not something conceived after the manner of a nature or further essential note. It adds no new categorizing feature to the thing. It makes the thing actual, for without it the thing is nothing. It can therefore be subsequently conceived as an act. When so conceptualized it turns out to be the notion of something which if a nature will have to be infinite and unique.[29] But it is not attained immediately by the intellect as a nature, but only as the act of a nature which is in some way other than that nature itself.

Accordingly, what is grasped in the judgment is only later conceptualized and gradually seen in its relation to the essence as act to potency.[30] The process, however, by which this relation is established, is long and intricate and surprisingly elusive. It apparently had little interest for the men of St. Thomas' day, and did not for the moment provide titles for ordinary or quodlibetal discussions, nor did it arise among the problems regularly treated in commenting upon the standard school texts. Actually, as far as one can trace it in the earliest writings of St. Thomas, the process by which he arrived at the primacy of existential act is complicated and difficult. What is immediately and directly known by the human intellect is the individual thing in the sensible world. Such things are thereby judged to exist in themselves, that is, in reality outside the mind. But by reflection the intellect sees those

same things existing in its own cognition.
The thing itself, or, if you wish, essence or
nature,[31] remains exactly the same; but its
existence in each of the two cases is different. This means that the same thing
can have different types of existence. It
can have existence in reality, and existence
in the mind. Both types are genuine, authentic existence, the one real, the other
cognitional or intentional. Since the same
essence may be found with the one or the
other existence, it is not bound down or
restricted to either.[32] In this way it is understood in its absolute consideration, in
which it abstracts from all being whatsoever. Considered absolutely in itself, it remains completely devoid of being.

But the essence does not prescind from
any of the existences which it is able to
have.[33] It cannot be considered apart from
its *order* to being, for that is what essence
means. It may prescind as well as abstract
from its individuating principles, or may
merely abstract without prescinding from

them.[34] In the latter case essence denotes the thing itself.[35] But it can never prescind from being. "Every nature is essentially a being."[36]

This is the doctrine of essence which is peculiarly characteristic of St. Thomas. All preceding philosophers, from Parmenides right through to Avicenna and William of Auvergne,[37] had taken for granted that a nature or essence or thing coincided with a being of its own. Parmenides on the rational plane could see no distinction between things and being. Plato had realized that the sensible things which confront human cognition were different from real being, but he allowed them some vague and image-like status of their own. Aristotle kept true being (being as being) apart from sensible things, yet saw in these some actual reality which could be related to true being and so allow them to be denominated beings. Plotinus had identified being with the intelligible natures themselves, trying to solve the difficulties by placing a One above being. But all these thinkers allowed the essence or nature some status, some type of being, in its own right, no matter what they called that being. The object that immediately confronted human conceptualization had for them all some kind of intelligibility or consistency of itself. In the Latin translations of Avicenna this appeared as the *esse proprium*,[38] the proper being of the thing; and in the controversies bearing explicitly on the difference between essence and existence, which arose so shortly after the death of St. Thomas, the essence as contrasted with existence was expressly of itself an object of intelligibility,[39] while from the time of Giles and Henry on, the notion of an *esse essentiae*, essential being distinct in some way from existence, became established in the Scholastic traditions.[40]

Nothing, in fact, could seem more obvious. If a thing had no being whatsoever, it just could not be known. Where there

was no being of any kind, there could not
be any cognoscibility at all. The object
just could not be known, it could not be
an object. Parmenides had been emphatic
on that point at the very beginning of
Greek metaphysical speculation. What is
and what can be known are the same.[41]
But the essence, according to a commonly
accepted Aristotelian description, was exactly the "what-is." It was the specifying
principle according to which a thing was
understood and placed in a category.

Yet St. Thomas is regarding the essence
just in itself as without any being whatever, and consequently without any intelligibility. Unlike other metaphysicians who
regard the essence in itself as the basic
principle of intelligibility in things, St.
Thomas sees it in none of the consistency
which makes an object intelligible. It is
neither one nor many,[42] it gives rise to no
truth.[43] Absolutely in itself it just cannot
be grasped by the intellect, for there is
nothing there to grasp! Only as already

having real being in the outside world, or as having cognitional being through the act of being known, can the essence function as a direct object of intellectual consideration. In itself, absolutely considered, the essence, contrary to the views of other types of metaphysics, has no being and no intelligibility at all.

In this way all being of every kind remains on the "existence" side of the "essence-existence" couplet. Being is other than essence. It is outside the essence, in the sense that it is not contained within the essential principles of finite things, nor does it follow from those principles in its own proper order of causality, namely efficient causality.[44] In this profound sense being is accidental to all things except in the unique though as yet hypothetical case of subsistent being.[45] But in another sense, equally profound and, from the emphasis laid upon it by St. Thomas,[46] at least equally important, being is essential to everything whatsoever. Actually, the essence is a nothing; yet potentially it is something. In this way, and in this way only, an essence differs from nothing. "Nothing" just cannot be, and essence on the other hand can be, it is of its very nature meant to be as far as its own formal causality is concerned. For that reason St. Thomas can say that every nature is essentially a being, that being follows *per se* upon form, that the being of a thing is as it were constituted by the principles of its nature.[47] In that formal sense being is not at all accidental to a thing, as St. Thomas insisted against Avicenna, but essential to it.

This combined accidental and essential character of being, involving being's absolute priority over essence, opens an astonishingly apt way toward the objectives that our culture requires of metaphysics. Because of its priority and accidentality to the sensible things themselves, the being of these things is seen through demonstration to have been received from something else and ultimately from sub-

sistent being. In this way the existence—
here a tautology[48]—and the nature of subsistent being is established. "Being" thereby appears as a nature different in reality
from any other nature, even though it is
found as a nature only in the unique instance of God. There alone being or existence is *what* exists, and so is a subsistent
nature. It is subsistent being.

The essential character of being, on the
other hand, requires that being follow
necessarily upon the principles of the form,
so that where the nature of a form, as in
the case of the human soul, is manifest in
activities independent of matter, then such
a soul cannot be separated from its being
any more than it can be separated from
itself—it is naturally incorruptible and im-
mortal.[49]

The Thomistic metaphysical principles,
accordingly, give rise to a procedure that
never has to make what critics of the demonstrations of God's existence call the "aw-
ful leap" from the finite to the infinite. The

Thomistic procedure makes no such jump. It never has to, for it does not start from a finite nature. It starts from the being of the thing, not as already submitted to the finitizing process of conceptualization, but as directly attained in the act of judgment. Proceeding from this starting-point, it establishes being as a nature and thereby has already reached the term of the demonstration. There is no question on the precisely metaphysical level of passing from a finite thing or a finite nature to an infinite one. The entire process is on the level of being, which as a nature or a thing is infinite, though it is attained not as a nature or a thing in the sensible world but as the act of a nature other than itself. That is why St. Thomas fails to see any difficulty in the objection that there is no proportion between the finite and the infinite, as in any way militating against the possibility of demonstrating God's existence. He answers that from *any* effect the *being* of its cause can be *manifestly* dem-

onstrated,[50] just as though such an objection had no place in a demonstration on
the level of being. On the other hand,
when the demonstration of God's existence
starts from the notion of being as already
conceptualized and so represented after
the manner of the original human concept
of act, which is limited in its intrinsic character quite as it was in its Aristotelian
equation with form, then St. Thomas is
just as insistent that no proof can be developed. The Anselmian argument is
worthless in the Thomistic framework.

Likewise, the demonstration of the
soul's immortality is firmly located on the
plane of being. It by-passes the collection
of unsatisfactory and inconclusive arguments on other planes, those for instance
of the *Phaedo*,[51] arguments that tend allur-
ingly toward their goal but somehow seem
to simmer out and vanish just as the goal
looms in sight.

Also, the Thomistic metaphysical procedure shows how being is really a nature,

different from any of the natures in the
finite world. Being is accordingly established as an actuality over and above the
other natures and so can constitute a genuine subject for a further science. It is far
from an empty concept. Rather, it is the
most meaningful of all. The subject of
Thomistic metaphysics is, of course, the
composite of essence and existence; for
that is what holds the priority in the gene-
sis of human thought.[52] But that subject is
constituted as such by the existential act.[53]
Existence as such, because it is not known
directly as a nature, cannot be the subject
of the science. Yet existence remains the
aspect[54] from which things are treated in
Thomistic metaphysics. It is the operative
character that extends the scope of the
science to everything which exists, either
really or intentionally, and so allows metaphysics to function in the broadest and
truest sense as a general science. It per-
mits metaphysics to use in its own right the
common principles of logic,[55] and so en-

ables it to judge the work of all other sciences from the one viewpoint which is common to all their objects, namely that of being.

Here, obviously, Thomistic metaphysics has an extremely complicated and difficult role. It has to learn in general the language of the different sciences which it encounters, it has to penetrate the nature of their thinking, it has to keep abreast of their progressive changes and development. In this respect, very evidently, it will never see its activity closed and final. Every radically new development in any of the other sciences will always place a fresh problem of interpretation before it. Likewise, every different type of metaphysics that arises has to be judged in a similar way.[56] Suffice it to say, then, that the approach from the viewpoint of existential act gives pre-eminently to the metaphysical doctrine of St. Thomas the means of exercising the difficult but necessary functions of a truly general science.

The Task

In these various ways, then, the Thomistic metaphysical doctrine gives full promise of meeting the needs that seem to guarantee the future of the science. However, as has been noted, no full-fledged metaphysics is to be found ready-made in the writings of St. Thomas. Unlike Suarez,[57] St. Thomas never had occasion later in life to interrupt his theological work and produce the huge treatises necessary to develop the metaphysical principles that he had been using all along in his theology. But in his text the principles are indeed to be found. The development is left for others. That is the task facing those devoted to Thomistic metaphysics today. It is a task that is neither easy nor simple.

First of all, there is the inevitable *purgative* way through which such endeavors have to pass. The men who inaugurated the nineteenth century revival of interest in Thomistic thought had themselves been trained in other types of philosophy. They could scarcely help but introduce alien and jarring elements into their new undertaking. Some of the most incompatible tenents have already been eliminated; for instance, common sense as a criterion of truth, the Wolffian division of the philosophical sciences, and the doctrine of the three fundamental truths of Balmes with its fatal requirement of a bridge between thought and reality. But numerous other such accretions, though already for the most part challenged, still remain to gnaw at the very roots of Thomistic vitality. The notion of essential being (*esse essentiae*) in some way distinct from existence, the reliance on a self-evident principle of causality as the ultimate basis for factual reasoning, the conception of an ontology capable of functioning apart from a natural theology, the illusion of direct perceptions[58] of essence and existence as really distinct principles of being, somewhat after the fashion of clear and distinct ideas,—all these and the like have still to be purged from metaphysical thinking that would call itself Thomistic. Like the idols that Francis Bacon[59] saw in the philosophical world of his day, they have to be thrown out of the Tribe, the Den, and the Market, or left to the Theatre of artificial constructions, no matter how attached to them our generation may have become.

Even the principle of identity has to be carefully submitted to the Thomistic criteria. The expression "principle of identity" does not occur in the writings of St. Thomas. If it is to be used at all in explaining his thought, it has to be understood according to his principles of being. The things from which human cognition takes its start are not perfectly self-identical.[60] They are not identical with their being, which is their most formal and most intimate characteristic.[61] Only God is perfectly self-identical, as far as essence and being are concerned. Accordingly, when one says "A is A," the subject, in Thomistic doctrine, is not perfectly self-identical with the predicate. The predicate includes the "is,"[62] that is, the being which is *other* than the subject. To express the identity of *a* being with its intelligible determination is to express that subject under the existential aspect from which its intelligible determination flows. That existential aspect, however, is the being which is other than the subject. The principle of identity, if it is to be used as a starting-point, can express only the very imperfect identity of a sensible thing with its being, an identity in which the aspect of otherness predominates.

However, careful as one must be in using expressions not found in the text of St. Thomas, especially those coined in alien philosophical atmospheres and presumably carrying with them the connotations of their original setting, this does not mean that all new terminology should be rigorously excluded. Rather, fresh terminology is to be welcomed if it helps to bring out more clearly the true meaning of

Thomistic doctrine. St. Thomas, after all, merely used the current philosophical vocabulary of his time. He did not invent a special one. "Existential act," for example, is not found in the text of St. Thomas, yet it neatly expresses the Thomistic meaning without importing any alien and incompatible thought.

Then, besides the purgative, an *illuminative* way still lies before the efforts at developing a Thomistic metaphysics. The scattered principles in the Thomistic text have to be focused in a way that will shed their full light upon the metaphysical problems concerning God and creatures,— for instance, on the notion of free-will, which the limiting and necessitating principles of essentialist philosophies cannot even approach; and also upon the intricate problems which metaphysics faces in its role of a general science. Here the task is tremendous. Descartes[63] had maintained that his own universal science would have to be the work of one man only, not of successive generations. But the task of bringing to perfection this illuminative process in Thomistic metaphysics would require a lifetime not merely of the allotted seventy years, but rather of the antidiluvian span of well over seven hundred! Even then the task will continue perennially as new and different problems arise with the course of progress and discovery.

It is a task, then, for the co-operative efforts of generations of scholars. So have the experimental sciences like physics and chemistry been developed. Actually, such is the way in which the work has been taking place during the past century, from both doctrinal and historical viewpoints and in the labor of textual critique. Though so much still lies ahead, and though there is as yet not the least room for complacency, the progressive results of a century of endeavor are nevertheless highly encouraging. One has but to look back at the continued advances registered for instance at each quarter century mark during the last hundred years. The contrast seen at each of these successive points is sufficient to drive away any lurking scepticism or discouragement!

With the illuminative stage, however, the comparison with the mystical life must end. There is here no unitive way. Unlike the Aristotelian, Thomistic metaphysics does not claim to offer man his beatitude. It does not unite him with his final end. It does not even reduce his knowledge to a perfect unity, but only to the ambiguity of man's first knowable, which is a composite of essence and existence. It proceeds only from the viewpoint of existence, leaving intact all starting-points in the realm of essence, both substantial and accidental. Accordingly, Thomistic metaphysics does not substitute for any of the other sciences, nor does it do any of their work, nor can it even enter into their proper fields. It does not provide salvation, and it does not exercise any imperialism over the other sciences. It itself teaches by its very na-

ture the humility that it requires in its
pursuer. It not only shows him how he
himself is of his nature a nothing, but also
that his intellect is specified and so graded
in intelligibility by an essence or quiddity
which similarly is of itself a nothing, namely, the quiddity of material things. It
makes him conscious of that lack of intelligibility and the need to go beyond it to the
act that makes the quiddity intelligible. To
really understand, the metaphysician has
to force his thought with difficulty along a
path which, though attainable, is above
the level on which his intellect functions
with ease,[64] and where the danger of error
is great and where comprehensive knowledge is impossible. The Thomistic metaphysician has to realize his limitations,
and nothing impresses them on him more
vividly than the very teaching of his science! He has, accordingly, one type of
work to do, and no other.

That work, from an obvious point of
view, may appear the least requisite of all.

As did Aristotle,[65] so the Thomistic metaphysician realizes that all the other arts
and sciences, which provide the necessi-
ties and amenities of life, have to come before his own. He will expect to see that
preference expressed in grants and schol-
arships and enticements to talent. De-
fense, construction, agriculture, the auto
business, the show business, the funeral
business and all other businesses will have
a prior claim on the general estimation of
his age.

Yet the need for establishing a strong
metaphysical tradition still remains for
those who will undertake it. To judge
from the lessons of history, those few will
never be lacking. In spite of all the limitations of metaphysics, the great need for
it will always remain, as well as its intrinsic worth and dignity. It is the science
of the highest objects naturally attainable
by man. It is the highest natural perfection of the highest human faculty. Though
not a life in itself, as it was for Aristotle, it

is still the highest vital activity possible on
the natural plane. St. Thomas has given
the principles required by that activity. It
is ours to develop them. *Noblesse oblige!*
That is the best honor we can pay the mas-
ter of human thought. It has been said
that the Thomistic doctrine may be com-
pared to the charismata, which were gifts
natural in character but extraordinary in
the way by which they were conferred. In
commemorating on his feast day the great
Christian doctor, we can render him no
more appropriate honor than by express-
ing publicly our consciousness of the
precious legacy that he has left us and our
duty of continuing to build on the founda-
tions that he has so solidly laid. In a word,
the metaphysical principles of St. Thomas
Aquinas open the way to the highest natural activity of the highest human faculty.
By emphasizing this tribute to his life-long
work we today do our modest part in continuing to ensure for his thought the pre-
eminent place envisaged by St. Albert,

and in so doing, as we contemplate the worth of the metaphysical inheritance which he has left us, we humbly return our thanks for the highest natural gift of God to men.

NOTES

1. ". . . et in fine conclusit, quod idem Fr. Thomas in scripturis suis imposuit finem omnibus laborantibus usque ad finem seculi, et quod omnes deinceps frustra laborarent." "Processus de Vita S. Thomae Aquinatis," c. IX, no. 82, in *Acta Sanctorum* (March), I, 712 F. The witness was Bartholomew of Capua, protonotary of the kingdom of Sicily. He testified to the narrative as told to him by the Dominican Hugo of Lucca, provincial prior of the Tuscan province, and so was giving it at second hand. One might perhaps be pardoned for suspecting that the original statement of the stolid German may possibly have been somewhat amplified in passing through the more exuberant southern minds.

2. Plato, *Sph.*, 248E-249A.

3. ". . . Paulum Apostolum, et postea Augustinum, et novissimo tempore dictum Fratrem Thomam, cui usque ad finem seculi non credebat alium successurum." *Acta Sanctorum, loc. cit.* (no. 83). On the Greek notion of "Successions" of philosophers, *cf.* R. D.

Hick's introduction to Diogenes Laertius, *Lives of Eminent Philosophers*, London and New York, 1925, I, xviii-xxvii.

4. ". . . existential Thomism . . . is neither whole or complete now nor will it ever constitute a closed and circumscribed system to which no addition can be made or in which no further depth is possible." R. J. Henle, *Method in Metaphysics*, Milwaukee, Marquette University Press, 1951, pp. 6-7. *Cf.* "Consequently any philosophical explanation, however sound and certain its positive elements may be, must remain open to deepening insight and the advancing conquest of reality." *Ibid.*, pp. 3-4. Also: "Le thomisme serait infidèle à ses propres origines si, par souci de fidélité à la tradition, il négligeait une source de lumière et de progrès, où qu'elle se trouve; or, chaque penseur digne de ce nom a quelque chose à nous apprendre." J. Pirlot, *L'Enseignement de la Métaphysique*, Louvain, Inst. Supér. de Philos., 1950, p. 120.

5. ". . . in Ontologia enodantur notiones maxime abstractae, utpote enti in genere convenientes, . . . Wolff, *Philosophia Prima sive Ontologia*, Prolegomena, 26. *Cf.*: "Istiusmodi notiones generales sunt notio essentiae, ex-

istentiae, ..." *Philosophia Rationalis sive Logica,* Discursus Praeliminaris, III, 73.

6. . . . so schien das sonderbare Schauspiel herbeigeführt zu werden, *ein gebildetes Volk ohne Metaphysik zu sehen;*—wie einen sonst mannigfaltig ausgeschmückten Tempel ohne Allerheiligstes. *Logik,* Preface to the first edition (1812).

7. *K. R. V.,* Preface to the first edition.—The metaphysics which Kant deplores is that of abstract notions and judgments, as exemplified in Wolff; *cf. Prolegomena to any Future Metaphysics,* 1-3. In another sense, however, Kant may allow his own critique to come under the general name of metaphysics; *cf.* K. R. V., A841 (B869).

8. *Metaph.,* A 2,982b9-10. The aspect of "ultimate," in the quest for the notion of metaphysics, is aptly underscored by A. E. Taylor: ". . . Metaphysics, because it is an attempt to find the right intellectual attitude toward *ultimate* reality, ..." *Elements of Metaphysics,* 13th ed., London, Methuen & Co., 1952, pp. xi-xii. *Cf.:* ". . . the special sciences deal each with some one particular aspect of things, and avowedly leave all ultimate questions on one side." *Ibid.,* p. 5.

9. *Cf.* P. Moraux, *Les Listes Anciennes des Ouvrages d'Aristote,* Louvain, éditions universitaires, 1951, pp. 312-315.

10. *Metaph.,* A 1,980a23 ff.

11. *Cf.* comment of E. Gilson, in *Newsweek* (Feb. 7, 1955), p. 51. The contemporary attitude has been well expressed in a recent editorial: "Le monde actuel est un monde par-dessus tout scientifique. Non certes que tous les hommes soient des savants; mais la civilisation dans laquelle nous vivons est impregnée de science. . . . Les masses certes n'expérimentent que les techniques; mais tout le monde cultivé suit avec passion les recherches des spécialistes." *Lumière et Vie,* XVII (1954), 3.

12. *Cf.* H. Bergson, *An Introduction to Metaphysics,* tr. T. E. Hulme, London, Macmillan, 1913.

13. *Cf.* R. G. Collingwood, *An Essay on Metaphysics,* Oxford, Clarendon Press, 1940, p. 47.

14. For Collingwood philosophy in general, as a species of literature, "represents the point at which prose comes nearest to being poetry." *An Essay on Philosophical Method,* Oxford, Clarendon Press, 1933, p. 213.

15. On this theme, *cf. E. Gilson's* Aquinas lecture *History of Philosophy and Philosophical Education*, Milwaukee, Marquette University Press, 1948.

16. *Cf. In Metaph.*, Prooem.; *In Boeth. de Trin.*, V, 4c; *In I Post. Anal.*, lect. 20, ed. Leonine, no. 6.

17. ". . . ens autem et essentia sunt que primo intellectu concipiuntur, . . ." *De Ente et Essentia*, Prooem., ed. M. -D. Roland-Gosselin, Paris, Vrin, 1926, p. 1. 3-4. ". . . et ideo terminus resolutionis in hac via ultimus est consideratio entis et eorum quae sunt entis in quantum huiusmodi." *In Boeth. de Trin.*, VI, 1 (ad 3m q.), ed. P. Wyser, Fribourg (Société Philosophique) & Louvain, E. Nauwelaerts, 1948, p. 60.31-33. "Illud autem quod primo intellectus concipit quasi notissimum, et in quo omnes conceptiones resolvit, est ens, . . ." *De Ver.*, I,1c, ed. R. Spiazzi, in *Quaest. Disp.*, Turin & Rome, Marietti, 1949, I,2b. "Primo autem in conceptionem intellectus cadit ens: quia secundum hoc unumquodque cognoscibile est, in quantum est actu, . . ." *S. Theol.* 1, 5, 2c, ed. Leonine.

18. "Sed in hoc differt, quod alterius scientiae,

scilicet inferioris, est scire ipsum *quia* tantum: . . . . Sed scire *propter quid* est superioris scientiae, ..." *In I Post. Anal.*, lect. 17, ed. Leonine, no. 3. "Unde oportet quod talis processus sit ex prioribus et ex magis notis simpliciter. . . . Et per consequens scientia superior erit magis scientia, quam inferior; et scientia suprema, scilicet *philosophia prima,* erit maxima scientia." *Ibid.*, no. 5. *Cf. In Boeth. de Trin.*, V,1, ad 9m; *ed. cit.*, p. 31.21-23. The technical terms and doctrines of *scientia propter quid* and *scientia quia* go back to Aristotle, *Anal. Post.*, I 13, 78a22 ff.

19. "Unde oportet quod ad eamdem scientiam pertineat considerare substantias separatas, et ens commune, quod est genus, cuius sunt praedictae substantiae communes et universales causae." *In Metaph.*, Prooem. *Cf. In Boeth. de Trin.*, V,4c.

20. *Cf. In Metaph.*, Prooem.

21. *E.g.:* "La théorie de l'Acte et de la Puissance ou de Mouvement est la clef de voûte de tout ce gigantesque édifice élevé, à la gloire de la philosophie spiritualiste, par le génie d'Aristote et de S. Thomas d'Aquin. A. Farges, *Théorie Fondamentale de l'Acte et de la Puissance,* 7th ed., Paris, 1909, p. 21.

22. *E.g.:* "A moins d'exclure Dieu de son objet propre et de cesser d'être générale, la métaphysique générale ne peut être charactérisée, comme science distincte, que par une unité simplement proportionelle. On comprend dès lors la portée de cette parole de Cajetan que nous citions plus haut: "Sine illa (notitia alalogiae) non potest metaphysicam quispiam discere." N. Balthasar, *L'Etre et les Principes Métaphysiques,* Louvain, Inst. Supér. de Philos., 1914, p. 67.

"Il semblerait que ces retentissements et ces applications devrait être innombrables, aussi vastes que l'être dont l'analogie est la fidèle acolyte; or, l'être est universel. Cependant, telle n'est point l'impression que nous donnent certains manuels modernes, écrits pourtant 'ad mentem Divi Thomae.' . . . En réalité il y a là une clé de voûte, une notion centrale et universelle, sans laquelle, impossible de rien comprendre à la métaphysique, . . ." M. T.-L. Penido, *Le Rôle de l'Analogie en Théologie Dogmatique,* Paris, Vrin, 1931, pp. 8-9.

23. *Cf.:* C. Fabro, *La Nozione Metafisica di Partecipazione,* 2nd ed., Turin, Società Editrice Internazionale, 1950; L.-B. Geiger, *La*

Participation dans la Philosophie de S. Thomas d'Aquin, Paris, Vrin, 1942; A. Little, *The Platonic Heritage of Thomism,* Dublin, Golden Eagle Books, 1951.

In applying this Platonic interpretation to the text of St. Thomas Aquinas, one should keep carefully in mind that the essence is for him something positive—*in re ponit* (*De Ente,* c. I; *ed. cit.,* p. 3.6). There is a tendency to speak of the limiting function of essence as though it were apparently negative in character, i.e., that it limits being through the role of "absence of more perfection." *E.g.:* "Therefore positive perfection and the absence of more perfection are opposed realities in the finite thing, or are really distinct." A. Little, *op. cit.,* p. 213. This seems to conceive being as limited somewhat after the fashion in which a white color or a surface is limited by its termini—it just stops going any further. One conceives it as a quiddity, of which one has just so much. Such limitation, no matter how one views it as connoting positive perfection, can hardly help but remain negative in its own proper character—its proper operative function is to ensure that there is *just* so much of the perfection in question, and *no* more, as in the case of the limitation by its

termini of a white color or a surface or anything else conceived as so limited.

But the limitation of being by essence is
considerably different. It is no longer merely
a question of having just so much being and
stopping suddenly. Quite evidently that
would amount to conceiving the being of
creatures as a "what," a quiddity, and making
it the "*what* is." *What* one had would be being, and just so much of it. This could hardly
help but run counter to the doctrine of the
De Ente et Essentia (*cf.* A. Little, *op. cit.*,
p. 193. Further on, this notion of "limit" was
explained by Fr. Little in a way that claims
to make it "simply positive"; *ibid.*, p. 210).
There the quiddity or "what" in finite things
is without exception other than their being.
Rather, unlike limitation by termini within
the order of essence, a limitation negative in
character, any limitation of being is *something* positive—*e.g.*, a stone, a tree, a man,
an angel. What properly constitutes the limitation of being in every case is the positive
content of these essences. In *being* positively
what it is, a stone or a tree or any other
finite thing limits that very being. The stone
or the tree, etc., is in fact that limitation.

By the same token, moreover, the limitation is not to be conceived as some *further* function of the essence, but just as the essence itself. It is not a negation which follows upon the already fully constituted essence, but is the very constitution of that essence, thereby as it were constituting the thing's being: "Esse enim rei quamvis sit aliud ab eius essentia, non tamen est intelligendum quod sit aliquod superadditum ad modum accidentis, sed quasi constituitur per principia essentiae." *In IV Metaph.*, lect. 2, *ed. cit.*, no. 558; *cf. infra,* n. 47. There can hardly be any question, then, of conceiving the being of creatures as a nature which is made to stop at the definite limits already set up by the finite essence. Rather, the only nature there is the finite quiddity, which is always other than its being, and with which it forms but one reality. Because it is a tree or a stone or some other positive finite nature, its being is the being of that restricted nature and of nothing else. The act or perfection of being is accordingly limited to and by the essence. But this limitation is not to be conceived after the manner of a form limited by a material subject, that is, in the line of material and formal causality; but rather from the viewpoint of a thing terminating the efficient causality which makes it exist, in contrast to the consideration that of its own nature it does not actually exist. In a word, the participation has to be conceived within the order of efficient causality, and not be allowed to lapse back into the order of formal causality in which the Platonic notion of participation originated. I have tried to show some of the implications of this consideration in "The Causal Proposition — Principle or Conclusion?", *The Modern Schoolman,* XXXII (1955), especially pp. 261-264 & 329.

In accordance with this doctrine, the being of creatures never becomes a "what," which could be conceived as limited because there is just so much of it there, even though things *are* exactly to the extent of the perfection required by their essences. In finite things the being of the thing is never *what* is there. Where being is found as a "what," *i.e.* in subsistent being, it is an essence or quiddity which is absolutely beyond the possibility of any limitation — "being" cannot be conceived as a nature of which one has just so much. Where being is found limited, it itself is never the nature with which one is dealing, and so is not to be conceived as functioning after the manner of a nature, even though one may be forced to speak of "the nature of being" as participated in all things. Being is a perfection, but a perfection which exhibits no conceptual content over and above the essence which it makes exist. As a limited perfection in creatures it certainly owes its limitation to the finite essence which it actuates. But that limitation is the positive character of the finite essence, and not at all a negation or a privation which could be explained within the nature of *being*. Parmenides is still a witness to the impossibility of any such attempt to account for the plurality of things.

These considerations show that both the essence and its being are positive, each in its own order. The positive character of the essence, like everything in the essence, is of course merely potential in itself, and is made actual only through its being. One has to avoid conceiving the essence first as fully constituted in itself, and then allowing it the further function of restricting a superadded perfection to the limits of its own already constituted self. But with this qualification, the reflection of D. J. B. Hawkins in *Being and Becoming*, London & New York, Sheed and Ward, 1954, p. 57, that essence is "a positive principle in its own right," may be admitted without hesitation of essence not only when essence is taken individually but also when it is considered universally.

24.   The existential interpretation of St. Thomas' doctrine, foreshadowed in J. Maritain's *Sept Leçons sur l'Etre,* Paris, Téqui, *n.d.* (1934), pp. 27-31, and E. Gilson's *Réalisme Thomiste et Critique de la Connaissance,* Paris, Vrin, 1939, pp. 219-227, was brought into prominence in the first and last chapters of the fifth edition of Gilson's *Le Thomisme,* 5th ed., Paris, Vrin, 1944, pp. 49-68, 505-520, and *Being and Some Philosophers,* Toronto, Pont. Inst. of Mediaeval Studies, 1949, as well as in Maritain's *Existence and the Existent,* New York, Pantheon Books, 1948. How the existential viewpoint involves the Thomistic doctrine of analogy and is required for the understanding of the participation problems, is neatly summed up by G. B. Phelan in his preface to J. F. Anderson's *The Bond of Being,* St. Louis, Herder, 1949. The doctrine of analogy, in fact, remains a very necessary metaphysical aspect which permeates the existential character of St. Thomas' doctrine of being. The contemporary reaction against the emphasis on it as the key to the interpre-

tation of Thomistic metaphysics goes much
too far when assigning it the status of merely
a "logical aid"; *e.g.*, ". . . St. Thomas only uses
the analogy of proportionality as a logical aid
in stating of God certain properties taken
from creation, *viz.*, in *De Ver.* 2.11. The analogy of proportionality must accordingly be
said not to play that central part in St.
Thomas, which is ascribed to him in Thomistic
quarters. H. Lyttkens, *The Analogy Between
God and the World,* Uppsala, Almqvist &
Wiksells, 1952, p. 475.

25. *Cf.*, on the one hand, Sartre's statement,
made of modern existentialists both Christian
and atheist, "What they have in common is
that they think that existence precedes essence, or, if you prefer, that subjectivity must
be the starting-point." *Existentialism,* tr. B.
Frechtman, New York, Philosophical Library,
1947, p. 15; and, on the other, that of St.
Thomas Aquinas: "Primus autem effectus est
ipsum esse, quod omnibus aliis effectibus
praesupponitur et ipsum non praesupponit
aliquem alium effectum; . . ." (*De Pot.*, III
4c; in *Quaest. Disp., ed. cit.,* II,46b). This
may be expressed as: ". . . the basic principle
of the existentialism of St. Thomas is that

the act of existence enjoys an absolute metaphysical priority over essence." J. F. Anderson, *The Cause of Being*, St. Louis, Herder,
1952, p. 140.

26. *E.g.: S. Theol.*, I,7; Prooem.; I,17,1 ad
2m; II-II, 111,3, ad 1m; III, 50,3, ad 4m;
In VII Metaph., lect. 17, ed. Spiazzi no. 1658;
ibid., VIII, 5, 1765. Verbal forms of *existere*, however, occur frequently.

27. The term *esse* in phrases like "Res ergo
composita non est suum esse" (*In de Hebd.*,
c. II; ed. Mandonnet, *Opusc.*, I, 175) can
hardly be translated by the English infinitive.
"Therefore a composite thing is not its own
'to be,'" is just not idiomatic. The notion
intended by St. Thomas in employing the
Latin infinitive is explained by him as follows: "Aliud autem significamus per hoc
quod dicimus esse, et aliud per hoc quod
dicimus id quod est; sicut et aliud significamus cum dicimus currere, et aliud per hoc
quod dicitur currens. Nam currere et esse
significantur in abstracto, sicut et albedo: sed
quod est, idest ens et currens, significantur
sicut in concreto, velut album"(*ibid.; ed. cit.*,
p. 171, except "Nam currere et *esse*," since
there is no justification for "currere et ens,"

at the beginning of the second sentence). *Esse* is meant to signify "abstractly," *in abstracto,* in contrast to terms which signify "concretely," *in concreto.* The basic model used for the contrast is the difference in signification between "whiteness" and "a white thing." This example illustrates the difference between "running" and "a runner." In English the participial form "running" signifies what St. Thomas understands as the notion *in abstracto,* and which in Latin he expresses either by the infinitive *currere* or the abstract noun *cursus* (ibid., p. 172; *cf. S. Theol.* I,50, 2, ad 3m). In Latin, on the contrary, the participial form *currens* signifies the one who is running, *i.e.,* it signifies *in concreto.* Applying these linguistical considerations to the translation of *esse* as a noun, one sees readily enough that the participial form "being" carries the same *in abstracto* signification as the Latin infinitive, and may safely be used to translate it.

28.   *Cf.:* "Cum in re duo sint, quidditas rei, et esse ejus, his duobus respondet duplex operatio intellectus. Una quae dicitur a philosophis formatio, qua apprehendit quidditates rerum, ... Alia autem comprehendit esse rei, . . ." *In I Sent.,* d. 38, q. 1, a. 3, Solut., ed. P.

Mandonnet, Paris, Lethielleux, 1929, I,903. "Prima quidem operatio respicit ipsam naturam rei. . . . Secunda vero operatio respicit ipsum esse rei, . . ." *In Boeth. de Trin.*, V,3c, ed. Wyser, p. 38.8-11. An instance of how far commentators in the first part of the present century were from regarding the judgment as the cognition of the most basic perfection in things may be seen in the following: "Il n'y a pas lieu de consacrer au jugement une étude spéciale, parce que le résidu qui lui appartient en propre, c'est-à-dire la simple affirmation d'une existence, n'a aucune valeur de spéculation pure." P. Rousselot, *L'Intellectualisme de Saint Thomas*, 2nd ed., Paris, Beauchesne, 1924, p. xvii, n. 1. *Cf.*: "Il paraît ici avoir confondu avec la certitude de l'affirmation la valeur de la spéculation pure. . . . C'était n'être pas fidèle aux principes de sa critique du jugement: la simple affirmation d'une existence n'a aucune valeur spéculative." *Ibid.*, p. 122, n. 1.

29.   *Cf. De Ente,* c. IV, ed. Roland-Gosselin, p. 34.15-30.

30.   *Cf. ibid.*, pp. 34.7-36.3. This procedure does not at all imply that the crucial metaphysical starting-point "would seem to be the real

distinction between essence and existence," as objected by R. McInerny in *Proceedings of the American Catholic Philosophical Association*, XXX (1956), 135. To commence with the consideration that being is not found within a finite thing's nature nor required by the principles of that nature, does not immediately show that the thing is *in reality* other than its being. The consideration, in fact, can be understood in a way which would result in the denial of any such distinction. Suarez, *D M*, XXXI, 6,23-24, ed. Vives, *Op. Om.*, XXVI, 250, for example, can look upon essence and existence as two different ways of conceiving the same thing, and admit a sense in which existence does not pertain to the essence of a creature; nevertheless, he can conclude with incontestable reasoning, given his own starting-point, that there is no "real distinction" between the two.

The Thomistic distinction, on the other hand, follows from considering the essence as of itself completely devoid of all being, real or intentional, and then reasoning to the reception of that being from something else and ultimately from subsistent being. Only then has being been established as a nature in reality, a nature that cannot coalesce *in reality* with any other nature, and so when participated is always other in reality than the nature which it makes be. In a word, the distinction in reality between a thing and its being can be demonstrated only after the existence and so the nature of God has been proven.

A "real distinction" in the sense so often found in commentators, namely, that of a distinction between two realities, is not found in the *De Ente et Essentia,* nor does it seem present anywhere in the authentic works of St. Thomas. Rather, the Thomistic distinction falls between the two entitative components of *every* finite reality, neither of which appears as a reality when considered just in itself. In other words, to have any reality whatsoever except subsistent being, one has to consider the two components as already present.

This consideration of sensible nature as of itself devoid of being and in potency to being is of course "properly a metaphysical consideration," *Proceedings of the American Catholic Philosophical Association, loc. cit.,* p. 136. It is the consideration of sensible nature from the viewpoint of its being, and not from that of its natural principles, matter

and form. To say that human metaphysics in
order to be meaningful has to be based upon
sensible things is entirely different from main-
taining that metaphysics has to be based
upon the conclusions of natural philosophy.

31. *Cf. infra,* n. 35.

32. *Cf. De Ente,* c. III, ed. Roland-Gosselin,
pp. 24.1-27.6. *Cf. De Pot.* V, 9, ad 16m; *ed.
cit.,* II,155a.

33. "Ergo patet quod natura hominis absolute
considerata abstrahit a quolibet esse, ita
tamen quod non fiat precisio alicuius eorum."
De Ente, loc. cit., p. 26.8-10.

34. *Ibid.,* c. II; pp. 12.5-23.7.

35. When abstracted with precision the essence
does not coincide with the individual material
thing — "essentia Socratis non est Socrates"
(*ibid.,* p. 23.7). But when abstracted without precision, the essence is predicated of the
individual thing and so is identical with
it: "dicitur enim Socratem esse essentiam,"
ibid., lines 5-6. In the latter sense, essence
may receive being in reality as well as in
cognition (*cf. ibid.,* pp. 24.1-25.8); so that to
speak of the distinction between essence or
nature on the one hand, and being on the
other, is the same as speaking of the distinc-

tion between a thing and its being. St. Thomas, *In I Sent.*, d. 8, q. 4, a. 2, ed. P. Mandonnet, Paris, Lethiellieux, 1929, I,222, moreover, has no hesitation in referring, after the manner of Avicenna, to *humanitas* as a nature which does not contain its being. The essence as abstracted with precision contains all the formal principles of the nature concerned. In the Aristotelian background, if being were contained in or followed from the principles of the nature, it would of course be sought only in the formal principles. *Cf.:* "In rebus enim materialibus tria est considerare, quorum nullum est aliud: scilicet individuum, naturam speciei et esse. Non enim possumus dicere quod hic homo sit sua humanitas, quia humanitas consistit tantum in speciei principiis; sed hic homo supra principia speciei addit principia individuantia, secundum quod natura speciei in hac materia recipitur et individuatur. Similiter etiam nec humanitas est ipsum esse hominis." *Q. de An.*, a. 17, ad 10m; in *Quaest. Disp.*, *ed. cit.*, II,346b.

36. ". . . quaelibet natura essentialiter est ens; . . ." *De Ver.*, I,1c; *ed. cit.*, I,2b. *Cf. ibid.*, XXI,1, arg. 1.

37. Regarding Avicenna, *cf. infra,* n. 38. For Williams of Auvergne: ". . . esse duas habet intentiones, et una earum est residuum a circumvestione et varietate accidentium, et hoc est proprie quod nominatur essentia, . . . et hoc est esse, quod diffinitio significat, . . ." *De Trin.,* c. II; Orleans-Paris, 1674, Supplementum, p. 2b.

38. "Et hoc est quod fortasse appellamus esse proprium; nec intendimus per illud nisi intentionem esse affirmativi, quia verbum ens signat etiam multas intentiones, ex quibus est certitudo qua est unaquaque res; et est sicut esse proprium rei." *Metaph.,* Tr. I, c. 6C, Venice, 1508, fol. 72vl.

39. *Cf.:* "Dicimus enim quod natura creata, licet sit tantae actualitatis quod possit per se intelligi: non sit tamen tantae actualitatis, quod possit existere in rerum natura, nisi superaddatur ei actualitas aliqua, quae communi nomine vocatur esse." Giles of Rome, *Quodl.,* V,3, Louvain, 1646, p. 273a. The argument that the essential predicates belong to a thing independently of its efficient cause became a standard argument for the "real distinction" between essence and existence. *E.g.:* "Ex quibus patet quod omnis propositio

de primo modo dicendi per se, et de secundo,
est necessaria et perpetuae veritatis. Cum
ergo quidditas rosae conveniat rosae in primo
modo dicendi per se, sequitur quod neces-
sario convenit ei. Quod etiam quidditas
rosae non conveniat ipsi rosae per aliquam
causam agentem extrinsecam, ita quod aliqua
causa efficiens sit causa quod rosa sit rosa,
ostendit Linconiensis." Capreolus, *Defensiones Theologiae D. Thomas Aquinatis, In
I Sent.*, 8,1,1, la concl., ed. Paban-Pégues,
Turin, 1900, I,303a. "Seclusa omni causalitate
effectiva respectu rosae, quaero an ista sit
vera, Rosa est substantia corporea; . . . si non,
ergo . . . praedicata primi modi possunt intelligi non ad esse (*sic*) rei, . . ." Cajetan, *In
De Ente et Essentia,* c. V; ed. M.-H. Lau-
rent, Turin, 1934, p. 157, (no. 100). "Esse
est receptum a causa efficiente, et ab ea de-
pendet in fieri et conservari, essentia vero per
se primo competit creaturae absque depend-
entia a causa efficienti: est enim perpetuae
veritatis, quod Petro conveniat esse homi-
nem. Quod autem Petrus existat, habet de-
pendenter a causa efficiente, ergo non potest
esse eadem res cum essentia." Bañes, *Scho-
lastica Commentaria,* in *S. Theol.* I,3,4, dub.
2, concl. 2, prob. 2, ed. L. Urbano, Madrid-

Valencia, 1934, I,147a. On the other side of
the controversy: "Et secundum hoc omnia
illa quae important res in rerum natura natas
existere dicuntur importare veras essentias
vel naturas sive quidditates de quibus vere
est scientia sive existant sive non existant,
. . . Unde rosa non existens videtur importare
veram essentiam praedicamentalem de genere
substantiae, non quod rosa ipsa actu sit illa
essentia vel sit substantia vel flos actu sive
quia actu habeat huiusmodi essentiam, sed
quia id quod nomine rosae apprehenditur
natum est esse actu in rerum natura secundum quod apprehenditur et iam est in po-
tentia et virtute suorum principiorum." God-
frey of Fontaines, *Quodl.* II,2, ed. De Wulf-
Pelzer, Louvain, 1904, p. 64. "Est enim essentia . . . id quo primo aliquid constituitur intra
latitudinem entis realis, ..." Suarez, *Disp.
Met.,* XXXI, 6,23, ed. Vives, Paris, 1856-1877,
XXVI, 250a.

On the Thomistic essence in this respect,
cf. G. Smith, "Avicenna and the Possibles,"
New Scholasticism, XVII (1943), 340-357.
Regarding the source of the intrinsic neces-
sity of essences, *cf.* W. Norris Clarke, "What
Is Really Real?," in *Progress in Philosophy,*
Milwaukee, Bruce, 1955, pp. 80-83.

40. *E.g.:* "et est hic distinguendum de esse secundum quod distinguit Avicenna in quinto in fine Metaphysicae suae, quod quoddam est esse rei quod habet essentialiter de se: quod appellatur esse essentiae. Quoddam vero quod recipit ab alio: quod appellatur esse actualis existentiae." Henry of Ghent, *Quodl.,* I,9, Paris, 1518, fol. 7r. ". . . esse, sive essentiae sive existentiae, quia unum non est sine altero, qualitercumque distinguantur . . ." John Duns Scotus, *Op. Ox.,* I,36,1, no. 11, ed. M. F. Garcia, Quaracchi, 1912, I,1177 (no. 1084). ". . . in creaturis esse essentiae et esse actualis existentiae differunt realiter, ut duae diversae res: . . ." Unknown author of the *Totius Logicae Summa,* Tr. II, c. 2, ed. Mandonnet, S. *Thomae Aquin. Opusc. Om.,* Paris, 1927, V,23. "Quia, sicut dicit Henricus, et bene meo judicio, essentia habet duplex esse, scilicet esse essentiae, et esse existentiae; . . ." Capreolus, *Defensiones,* in *II Sent.,* 1,2,3, *ed. cit.,* III, 76a. ". . . esse est duplex, scilicet existentiae et essentiae, . . ." Cajetan, *In De Ente et Essentia,* c. V; *ed. cit.,* p. 158 (no. 101). ". . . esse essentiae creaturae ut sic ex se praescindit ab esse actuali extra causas, quo res creata fit extra nihil, quod nomine esse existentiae actualis significamus."

Suarez, *Disp. Met.*, XXXI,1,2; *ed. cit.*, XXVI, 225a. On *esse essentiae* and *esse existentiae* in Giles of Rome, *cf.* forthcoming article of P. Nash, "The Accidentality of *Esse* according to Giles of Rome," published in the *Gregorianum,* January, 1957.

41. Fragment 3 (Diels-Kranz, *Fragm. Vorsok.*). *Cf.* Frs. 6.1 and 8.34. On the meaning of these fragments, *cf.* K. v.Fritz, "ΝΟΤΣ, ΝΟΕΙΝ and their Derivatives in Pre-Socratic Philosophy," *Classical Philology* XL (1945), 237-238.

42. "Unde si queratur utrum ista natura sic considerata possit dici una uel plures neutrum concedendum est, quia utrumque extra intellectum humanitatis, et utrumque potest sibi accidere." *De Ente*, c. III, ed. Roland-Gosselin, p. 24.10-13.

43. ". . . ratio veritatis fundatur in esse, et non in quidditate, . . ." *In I Sent.*, d. 19, q. 5, a. 1, ad 7m, ed. Mandonnet, I,489. *Cf. De Ver.*, I,1, ad 3m in contr., ed. Spiazzi, I,4a. In the existentialism of St. Thomas, accordingly, there is no objectivity except through existential act, real or intentional. This priority of existence over the objective is of course radically different from the corresponding priority in modern existentialism. Because it

locates in God the source of existence and thereby of goodness, it occasions not anxiety or frustration or despair, but rather virtues like humility and hope, the kind of virtues so despised by the rationalistic tradition against which modern existentialism revolted—*e.g.*: "Celibacy, fasting, penance, mortification, self-denial, humility, silence, solitude, and the whole train of monkish virtues; for what reason are they everywhere rejected by men of sense, but because they serve to no manner of purpose; neither advance a man's fortune in the world, nor render him a more valuable member of society; . . ." Hume, *Enquiries,* IX,1,219, ed. Selby-Bigge, Oxford, 1902, p. 270.

The complete lack of being in the natures of the things known in human cognition, moreover, is what guarantees the genuine objectivity of that cognition. If the thing were identified in reality with any kind of being, it could not assume a different kind of being in cognition without thereby undergoing a change in its very nature, and so rendering uncontrollable the objectivity of human cognition.

44.   *Cf. De Ente,* c. IV; *ed. cit.,* p. 35.6-8.

45. In the procedure followed in *De Ente et Essentia* St. Thomas first (c. IV; p. 34.15-30) shows that if there is subsistent being, that is, something whose quiddity is existence, such being cannot undergo plurification either in singulars or in species. All other being will be participated in secondary instances, and will remain other than the quiddity or nature of those instances. Accordingly, if there is subsistent being, it will be unique and primary. This procedure, consequently, is hypothetical and inchoative. Only later (*ibid.*, p. 35.6-19) does the treatment show that subsistent being actually exists, *i.e.*, that being is a nature which subsists in that unique and primary instance.

46. *Cf. supra*, n. 36. It is this aspect of being, taken over from Aristotle, that St. Thomas defends emphatically against Avicenna. *Cf.* St. Thomas, *In IV Metaph.*, lect. 2, ed. Spiazzi, nos. 556-558; *In X Metaph.*, lect. 3, nos. 1981-1982.

47. "Esse enim rei quamvis sit aliud ab ejus essentia, non tamen est intelligendum quod sit aliquod superadditum ad modum accidentis, sed quasi constituitur per principia essentiae." *In IV Metaph.*, lect. 2, ed. Spiazzi,

no. 558. ". . . esse per se consequitur formam creaturae, supposito tamen influxu Dei: sicut lumen sequitur diaphanum aeris, supposito influxu solis." *S. Theol.*, I,104,1, ad 1m, ed. Leonine. *Cf.*: Per hoc enim in compositis ex materia et forma dicitur forma esse principium essendi, quia est complementum substantiae, cuius actus est ipsum esse: sicut diaphanum est aeri principium lucendi quia facit eum proprium subiectum luminis. *CG*, II,54, ed. Leonine, XIII,392a20-25. This comparison shows clearly how St. Thomas conceives the principles of the essence as causing being only in the line of formal causality, and even then presupposing the efficient causality of the agent. So: ". . . esse naturale per creationem Deus facit in nobis nulla causa agente mediante, sed tamen mediante aliqua causa formali: forma enim naturalis principium est esse naturalis." *De Ver.*, XXVII,1, ad 3m, ed. Spiazzi, I,512b. ". . . Deus esse naturale creavit sine medio efficiente, non tamen sine medio formali. Nam unicuique dedit formam per quam esset." *De Car.*, a. 1, ad 13m; *ed. cit.*, II,756b.

48.   To say that subsistent being is a real nature is to mean that it actually exists. Both sub-

ject and predicate coincide in meaning in the
statement: "Subsistent being exists."

49. "Manifestum est enim quod id quod secundum se convenit alicui, est inseparabile ab
ipso. Esse autem per se convenit formae,
quae est actus. . . . Impossibile est autem,
quod forma separetur a seipsa. Unde impossibile est quod forma subsistens desinat
esse." S. *Theol.* I,75,6c, ed. Leonine.

50. ". . . per effectus non proportionatos causae,
non potest perfecta cognitio de causa haberi:
sed tamen ex quocumque effectu potest mani-
feste nobis demonstrari causam esse, ut dictum est. Et sic ex effectibus Dei potest demonstrari Deum esse: . . ." S. *Theol.* I,2,2, ad
3m, *ed. cit.*

51. *Phd.* 70A-107B.

52. St. Thomas consistently speaks of the subject of metaphysics as *ens* or *entia,* in the
sense of the things which are. "Sed Philoso-
phus primus considerat de rebus secundum
quod sunt entia; . . ." *In VII Metaph.,* lect.
13, ed. Spiazzi no. 1576. *Cf. In Metaph.,*
Prooem.; *In IV Metaph.,* lect. 1-5 *passim;*
In XI Metaph., lect. 3-4; *In Boeth. de Trin.,*
V, 4c. *Ens* in the sense of *that which is* is a

composite of essense and being; *cf. De Ente,*
Prooem. and c. I.

53. "Ratio autem entis ab actu essendi sumi-
tur, non autem ab eo cui convenit actus essendi, ..." *De Ver.,* I,1, ad 3m in contr.; ed.
Spiazzi, I,4a.

54. Because for St. Thomas the "existential
aspect" is an act other in reality than the nature of things, it is able to give rise to a distinct science. This Thomistic view is quite
different from such modern conceptions as:
". . . every philosophical science partakes of
the nature of metaphysics, which is not a
separate philosophical science but a special
study of the existential aspect of that same
subject-matter whose aspect as truth is studied
by logic, and its aspect as goodness by ethics."
R. G. Collingwood, *Philosophical Method,* p.
127. Gilson observes: "As one conceives being, so one will conceive metaphysics." *History of Philosophy and Philosophical Education,* p. 32.

55. "Et sic dicetur aliquis processus esse ration-
abilis, quando aliquis utitur in aliqua scientia
propositionibus, quae traduntur in logica,
prout scilicet utimur logica, prout est docens
in aliis scientiis. . . . Convenit autem hoc

proprie et convenienter fieri in logica et meta-
physica eo quod utraque scientia communis
est et circa idem subiectum quodammodo."
In Boeth. de Trin., VI,1c ad 1m q., ed. Wyser,
p. 56.4-10.

56. Because of its profound penetration of
reality and thought in its character of a general science, Thomistic metaphysics is able
to provide a deeply sympathetic understanding of other metaphysical procedures. It
shows how Parmenides had to reason consistently to his extreme conclusions, once he
had refused even to express any distinction
between things and their being. It manifests
the nature of the perennial Platonic difficulties in attempting to assign any definite type
of being to forms taken just in themselves,
and therefore according to their absolute consideration, in which they exhibit no being
whatsoever. It reveals why the Aristotelian
metaphysics, locating being ultimately in
form, had to remain open to a multiplicity
of finite pure acts, and could not arrive at a
pure act that would be unique and infinite.
It realizes just what is happening when philosophical procedures, like most of those from
Descartes on, commence with natures identi-

fied with a secondary type of being, the cognitional. Because it is aware of what is taking place in these procedures, it is able to assess them critically and profit by whatever light their consistent reasoning and penetrating observations may throw on metaphysical problems, for it sees just what type of being is contained or not contained in their starting-points.

Nor is this failing to approach other philosophies in an "objective" fashion. One cannot approach them in an intellectual vacuum. If one uses their principles as starting-points, one inevitably has to accept their conclusions. If one cannot accept those conclusions, one necessarily has to use different principles to assess the philosophical procedure involved. This is a role that the Thomistic metaphysical principles are pre-eminently able to play. Their universality, as universal as being itself, allows and should compel their proponents to treat with the broadest of understanding and with delicate sensitivity all genuine philosophical positions other than their own. It is no longer fashionable for an exponent of Thomistic metaphysical doctrine to dismiss such positions with a "toto caelo errat," or to engage in *refuting* them after the manner of theological procedure. His task is to *understand* them. The rest, on the philosophical plane, takes care of itself. *Cf. supra,* n. 4.

57. *Cf. Disp. Met.,* Ad Lectorem; in *Op. Om.,* ed. Vives, XXV, *init.*

58. This seems to be the case with those who take the first part (*De Ente,* c. IV, ed. Roland-Gosselin, p. 7-15) of the long argument of St. Thomas and isolate it as a separate proof for a "real distinction" between essence and existence in creatures. Because one can know what a man or a phoenix is without knowing that any such thing exists in reality, one is supposed to see that the being is in reality other than the essence. Such an understanding of the argument would seem to take for granted that one has a direct and immediate perception of the essence as a reality complete and rounded-off in itself, as though it prescinded from being, and a similar perception of existence as a distinct reality. This has been called the "logical proof" of the real distinction. But as found in St. Thomas, it does not enter the logical order at all. It starts from the nature considered absolutely, and so as *common* to both the logical and real orders, and proper to neither. From that

starting-point it proceeds at once to the real
order. Wherever this argument is found in
St. Thomas, it either leads up to the demonstration of subsistent being (*De Ente, loc.
cit.*), or occurs after the existence of God
has been proven and so after being has already been established as a nature in reality,
In II Sent., d. 3, q.1, a.1, Solut., ed. Mandonnet, II,87. *CG*, I,22; ed. Leonine, XIII,
68a5-24. *S. Theol.* I,3,5c. *Comp. Theol.*, c. XI.

59. *Novum Organon*, I,39-68.

60. "Aliquando autem ex his quae simul jung-
untur, non resultat res tertia, sed resultat
quaedam ratio composita; sicut ratio hominis
albi resolvitur in rationem hominis et in
rationem albi; et in talibus aliquid componi-
tur ex se ipso et alio, . . ." *Quodl.*, II, 3, ad
1m, ed. P. Mandonnet, Paris, Lethielleux,
1926, p. 43. This is in reply to the argument:
"Si ergo Angelus componeretur ex essentia
et esse, componeretur ex se ipso et alio. Hoc
autem est inconveniens." *Ibid.*, p. 42.

61. "Esse autem est illud quod est magis inti-
mum cuilibet, et quod profundius omnibus
inest: cum sit formale respectu omnium quae
in re sunt, . . ." *S. Theol.* I,8,1c. ". . . esse
est illud quod immediatius et intime con-

venit rebus, . . ." *Q. de An.*, a. 9, init.; *ed. cit.*, II,314a.

62. ". . . in talibus, *est*, praedicatur ut adiacens principali praedicato. . . . simul cum nomine praedicato facit unum praedicatum, . . ." *In II Periherm.*, lect. 2, ed. Leonine, no. 2. *Cf.* Appendix in 2nd ed., Toronto, 1952, of Gilson's *Being and Some Philosophers*, pp. 224-227. Gilson (*op. cit.*, p. 15) stresses the "fundamental ambiguity of the word *'being'*." St. Thomas noted the deception that had arisen "ex aequivocatione entis." *In X Metaph.*, lect. 3, *ed. cit.* no. 1982.

63. *Discours de la Méthode*, 2e partie, (*A-T*) VI, 11.12-12.25; and 6e partie, p. 72.16-19.

64. *Cf.* H. Bergson, *Introduction to Metaphysics*, *ed. cit.*, pp. 56-59. E. Gilson, *Le Thomisme*, 5th ed., 1944, pp. 60-61.

65. *Metaph.*, A 1-2, 980a22-983a11.

The Aquinas Lectures

Published by the Marquette University Press,
Milwaukee 3, Wisconsin

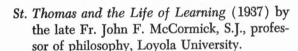

St. Thomas and the Life of Learning (1937) by
the late Fr. John F. McCormick, S.J., professor of philosophy, Loyola University.

St. Thomas and the Gentiles (1938) by Mortimer J. Adler, Ph.D., associate professor of the
philosophy of law, University of Chicago.

St. Thomas and the Greeks (1939) by Anton C.
Pegis, Ph.D., president of the Pontifical Institute of Mediaeval Studies, Toronto.

The Nature and Functions of Authority (1940)
by Yves Simon, Ph.D., professor of philosophy of social thought, University of Chicago.

St. Thomas and Analogy (1941) by Fr. Gerald
B. Phelan, Ph.D., director of the Mediaeval
Institute, University of Notre Dame.

St. Thomas and the Problem of Evil (1942) by
Jacques Maritain, Ph.D., professor of philosophy, Princeton, University.

Humanism and Theology (1943) by Werner
Jaeger, Ph.D., Litt.D., "University" professor,
Harvard University.

The Nature and Origins of Scientism (1944) by Fr. John Wellmuth, S.J., chairman of the department of philosophy, Xavier University.

Cicero in the Courtroom of St. Thomas Aquinas (1945) by the late E. K. Rand, Ph.D., Litt.D., LL.D., Pope professor of Latin, *emeritus,* Harvard University.

St. Thomas and Epistemology (1946) by Fr. Louis-Marie Regis, O.P., Th.L., Ph.D., director of the Albert the Great Institute of Mediaeval Studies, University of Montreal.

St. Thomas and the Greek Moralists (1947, Spring) by Vernon J. Bourke, Ph.D., professor of philosophy, St. Louis University, St. Louis, Missouri.

History of Philosophy and Philosophical Education (1947, Fall) by Étienne Gilson of the *Académie française,* director of studies and professor of the history of mediaeval philosophy, Pontifical Institute of Mediaeval Studies, Toronto.

The Natural Desire for God (1948) by Fr. William R. O'Connor, S.T.L., Ph.D., professor of dogmatic theology, St. Joseph's Seminary, Dunwoodie, N.Y.

St. Thomas and the World State (1949) by Robert M. Hutchins, Chancellor of the University of Chicago.

Method in Metaphysics (1950) by Fr. Robert J. Henle, S.J., dean of the graduate school, St. Louis University, St. Louis, Missouri.

Wisdom and Love in St. Thomas Aquinas (1951) by Étienne Gilson of the *Académie française,* director of studies and professor of the history of mediaeval philosophy, Pontifical Institute of Mediaeval Studies, Toronto.

The Good in Existential Metaphysics (1952) by Elizabeth G. Salmon, associate professor of philosophy in the graduate school, Fordham University.

St. Thomas and the Object of Geometry (1953) by Vincent Edward Smith, Ph.D., professor of philosophy, University of Notre Dame.

Realism and Nominalism Revisited (1954) by Henry Veatch, Ph.D., professor of philosophy, Indiana University.

Imprudence in St. Thomas Aquinas (1955) by Charles J. O'Neil, Ph.D., professor of philosophy, Marquette University.

The Truth That Frees (1956) by Fr. Gerard Smith, S.J., Ph.D., professor and director of the department of philosophy, Marquette University.

St. Thomas and the Future of Metaphysics (1957) by Fr. Joseph Owens, C.Ss.R., associate professor of philosophy, Pontifical Institute of Mediaeval Studies, Toronto.

Uniform format, cover and binding.